Stay Away! Come Here!

CONTENTS

NATIONAL GEOGRAPHIC School Publishing
Hampton-Brown

Prefixes un-, re-, mis-

Look at each picture. Read the words.

Example:

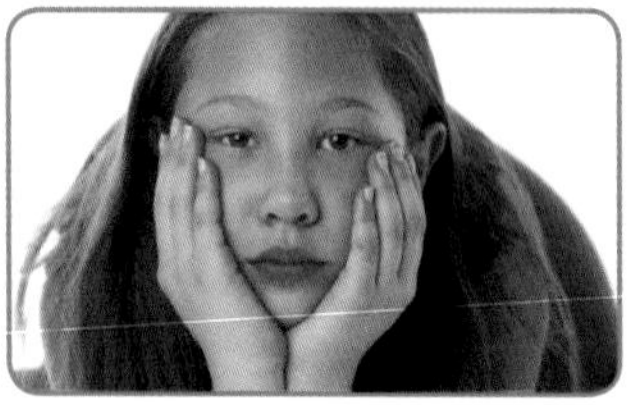

unhappy

unload

repaint

rewrite

misbehave

misspell

High Frequency Words

- animal
- ball
- eye
- few
- food
- large
- might
- move
- number
- often

Key Words

Look at the pictures. Read the sentences.

Hunt!

1. The **eye** of the **animal** glowed like a gold **ball**.
2. It waited a **few** moments and then made a quick **move** to catch its **food**.
3. It **might** take all night to catch a **large** **number** of ants.
4. It does not **often** go to sleep hungry!

Phonics Games
NGReach.com

Spikes and Scales!

by Mary Bendix

When you go out, open your eyes and look. Our planet is filled with large numbers of fantastic animals. You are about to meet one of them.

Is this animal misnamed?

People often call this animal a horned toad. They need to rethink that name. It's wrong! The right name for this misnamed animal is horned *lizard*.

A toad	A horned lizard
is not a reptile.	is a reptile.
lays eggs in ponds and lakes.	lays eggs on land.
has dry, warty skin but no scales.	has dry skin with scales.

Yes, it might seem to be a toad. Its flat nose and large belly give it a toad shape. But a lizard is unlike a toad in a few ways. Some can be seen, and some are unseen. Some ways are shown in the chart above.

What places do horned lizards call home?

Horned lizards like hot, dry places. Many animals are unable to survive in the desert, but horned lizards feel at home there.

How do horned lizards stay safe?

Horned lizards blend in with the land. If it does not move, animals hunting for food mistake the lizard for a rock.

What do horned lizards eat?

A horned lizard eats ants. It can react fast when an ant runs past. Snap! The ant has no time to retrace its steps. Gulp! It takes many ants to fill that large belly.

What makes life hard for horned lizards?

Horned lizards are in danger. Many places where horned lizards live are unprotected. The land is cleared. Houses and shops replace the lizards' desert homes. The lizards cannot relocate to safer spots.

People protect themselves while spraying.

Roads cut the land. Horned lizards are unable to move fast. They cannot dodge traffic that zips past when they are basking in the sun.

People spray and respray to get rid of pests such as ants. If there are no ants to eat, the horned lizards cannot find food.

People also mistreat and misuse horned lizards. They often try to keep them as pets. Most horned lizards cannot survive if they are not in the wild. Many states do not let people keep them.

A horned lizard faces another danger. It is hunted by snakes and foxes.

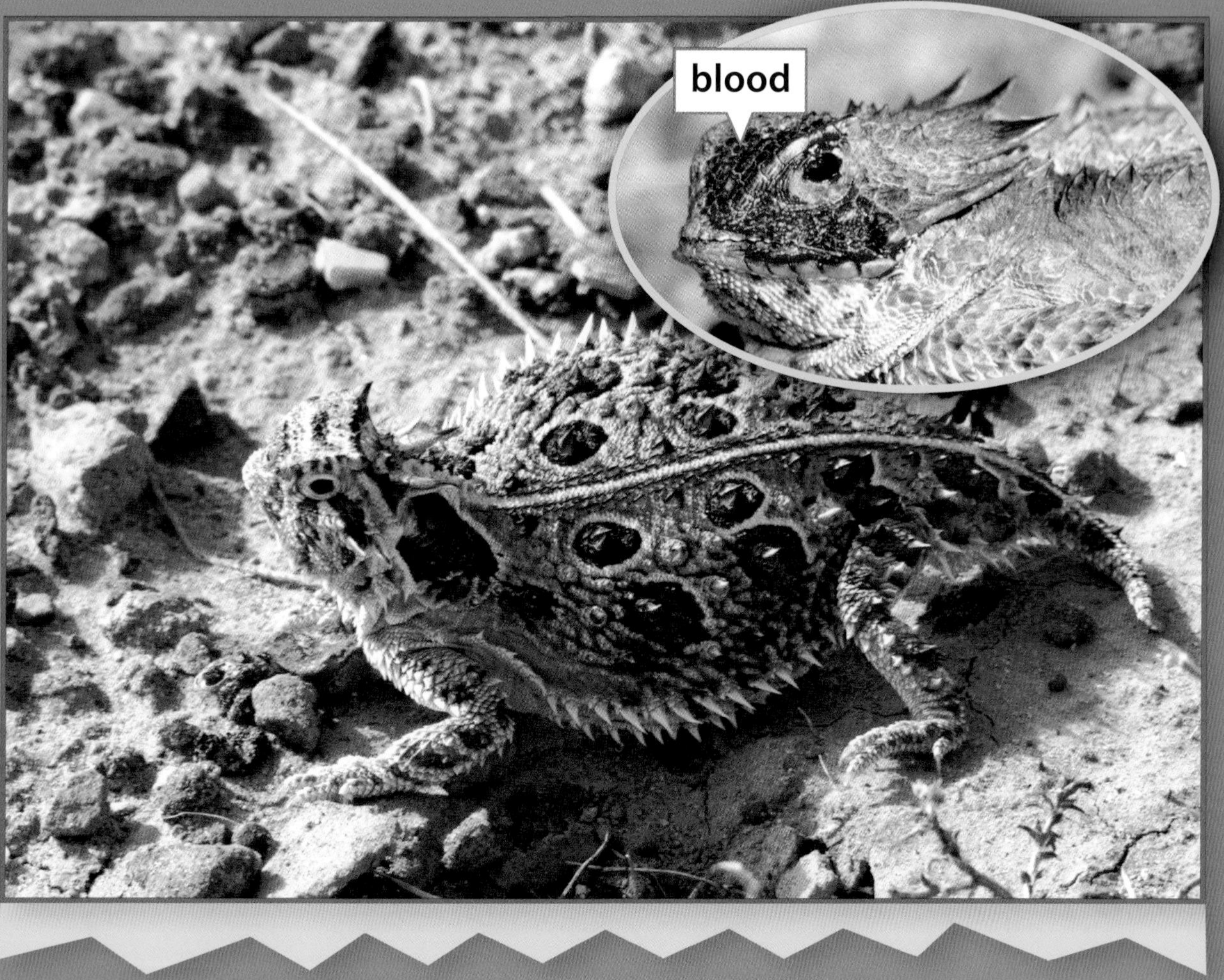

How do horned lizards react to danger?

The horned lizard can puff up like a soccer ball. Hunters may be unwilling to eat a soccer ball with spikes.

It can also squirt blood out of its eyes! Hunters do not misunderstand what this means: *Stay back!*

What is best for a horned lizard?

Horned lizards belong in the wild. They need safe, sunny spots. They need land filled with rocks, so they can move unseen from place to place. And they need lots of ants to eat! ❖

Prefixes un-, re-, mis-

Read these words.

minus	unseen	reshape	mismatch	safe
unsafe	rethink	using	mistreated	unprotected

Find the words with the prefixes **un**-, **re**-, or **mis**-. Use letters to build them.

u n s a f e

Talk Together

Choose words from the box above. Tell your partner if each desert animal next to the arrow is safe or unsafe.

This unseen animal is safe.

Suffixes -**y**, -**ly**, -**ful**

Look at each picture. Read the words.

Example:

stink**y**

quick**ly**

thirst**y**

play**ful**

stick**y**

grace**ful**

High Frequency Words
animal
ball
eye
few
food
large
might
move
number
often

Key Words

Look at the pictures. Read the sentences.

Collecting Pollen

1. The **eye** of a daisy is like a black **ball**.
2. **Animals** such as bees **move** from bud to bud, collecting pollen as **food**.
3. It **might** take a **few** trips to collect **large** globs of pollen.
4. Bees **often** must go a **number** of miles to find food.

Phonics Games
NGReach.com

Plant Helpers

by Rose Wagner

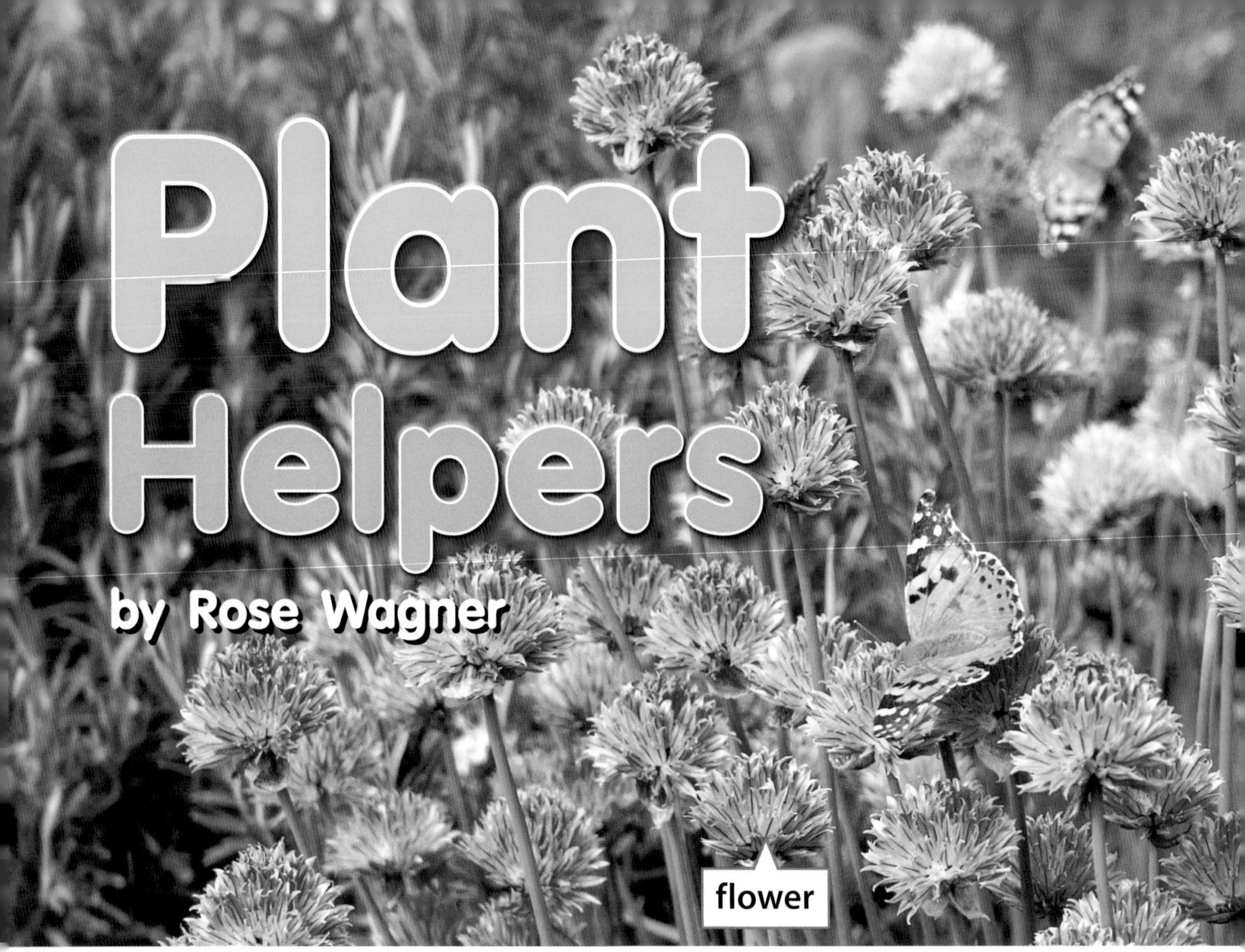

What Plants Need

A plant cannot survive unless it has a few important things:

1. A plant needs dirt.

2. A plant needs water.

3. A plant needs sunshine.

Plants don't have babies. Instead, they need to scatter pollen from flower to flower. But it cannot move! It is firmly rooted! It must depend on helpful insects, birds, and other animals. These helpers are called pollinators.

Help Wanted

How do plants get pollinators to help? Plants use flowers.

What do you think of when you think of a flower? You might think of its smell. Flowers can often smell sweet or spicy or fruity or stinky! These smells can bring helpers.

You might remember how bright flowers are. Flowers can be a paint box of shades. The sharp eyes of helpers spot these bright shades. So eye-catching flowers can bring helpers.

You might remember how graceful flowers are. Flowers can be a number of shapes, such as balls, bells, trumpets, and cups. Flower shapes can bring helpers.

Scattering Pollen

Flowers have a sweet, sticky juice called nectar. Hungry helpers come to sip the nectar. Grains of pollen stick to them. When they fly or creep to the next flower, they take the pollen with them.

Insect Helpers

Pollinators include insects such as bees, butterflies, and ants, to name a few. Flying is a helpful skill for a pollinator to have. Flying insects can quite quickly visit a large number of flowers.

Bird Helpers

Lots of pollinators depend on flowers for food. Bright flowers bring hummingbirds. These flowers can be shaped like cups or trumpets. Sharp beaks can dip deeply inside. A hummingbird sips tasty nectar and gets dusted with pollen.

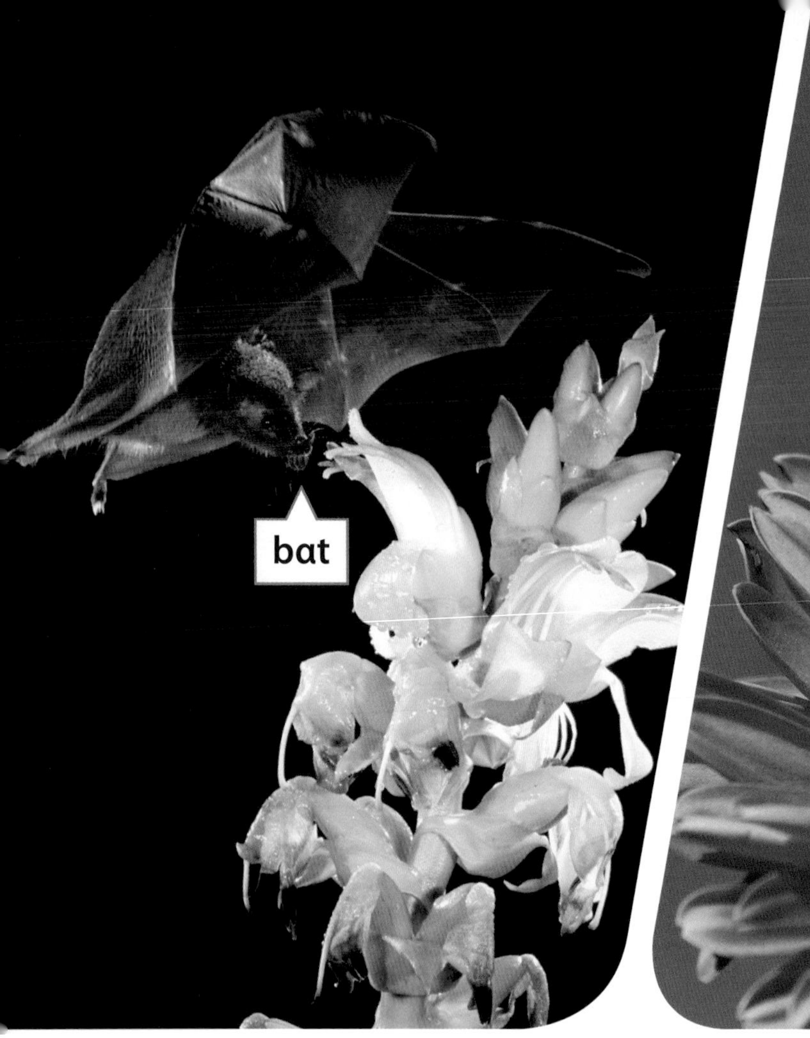

Other Animal Helpers

Bats, lizards, and a few other animals are pollinators. Here's what they do:

- Bats make nightly trips to large white flowers that smell fruity or stinky. Lots of fruits depend on bat pollinators.
- Thirsty lizards sip nectar. Pollen sticks to scaly skin.

• Climbers such as possums and bush babies can easily reach flowers in leafy trees. These plant helpers can use long tongues, sharp nails, and clingy, curly tails. Pollen sticks to feet, noses, and furry faces.

Thanks to large numbers of plants, many animals can get food from flowers. Thanks to helpful pollinators, new plants can grow. ❖

Suffixes -y, -ly, -ful

Read these words.

really	jumpy	fluttery	helpful	graceful
fluffy	quickly	painful	playful	fuzzy

Find the words with the suffixes –**y**, –**ly**, or –**ful**. Use letters to build them.

f l u f f y

Talk Together

Choose words from the box above to tell your partner about this garden in a park.

This animal is really fuzzy and painful.

Pollinate!

Pretend you are a bee. Follow this path to find food in the garden and get home quickly.

1. Move past the fluffy, unhappy animal.
2. Stop at the large, droopy flowers.
3. Get some refreshing, tasty food at the blossom with the big black eye.
4. Retrace your flight to buzz over the misplaced, beach ball.
5. Go past the graceful animal made of stone.
6. Follow the rocky path to return home quickly.

Acknowledgments
Grateful acknowledgment is given to the authors, artists, photographers, museums, publishers, and agents for permission to reprint copyrighted material. Every effort has been made to secure the appropriate permission. If any omissions have been made or if corrections are required, please contact the Publisher.

Photographic Credits
CVR (b) Steve Byland/Shutterstock. (t) Bill Draker/imagebroker/age fotostock. **3** Liz Garza Williams/Hampton-Brown/National Geographic School Publishing. **4-5** Gordon & Cathy Illg/Animals Animals. **6** Kirsanov/Shutterstock. **7** Derrick Hamrick / Rolfnp/Alamy Images. **8** George Grall/National Geographic Image Collection. **9** Michael and Patricia Fogden/Minden Pictures/National Geographic Image Collection. **10** Ron Chapple/Corbis. **11** Ingram Publishing/Photolibrary. **12** Kenneth Garrett/National Geographic Image Collection. **13** (inset) John Cancalosi/Peter Arnold, Inc. (t) John Sullivan/Ribbit Photography. **14** Jeremy Woodhouse/Getty Images. **15** Liz Garza Williams/Hampton-Brown/National Geographic School Publishing. **16** (bl) Alan G. Nelson/Animals Animals. (br) Roy Toft/National Geographic Image Collection. (cl) Gallo Images-Heinrich van den Berg/Getty Images. (cr) Art_man/Shutterstock. (tl) PhotoDisc/Getty Images. (tr) James Urbach/SuperStock. **17** Liz Garza Williams/Hampton-Brown/National Geographic School Publishing. **18-19** Bill Philpot/Alamy Images. **19** (tr) J. Baylor Roberts/National Geographic Image Collection. **2** (bl) Corbis/SuperStock. (cl) RubberBall/SuperStock. (cr) Mike Flippo/Shutterstock. (tl) Stockbyte/Getty Images. (tr) Comstock/Getty Images. **20** (cc, tl) PhotoDisc/Getty Images. (tr) Stockbyte/Getty Images. **21** (cc) PhotoDisc/Getty Images. (tl) Stockbyte/Getty Images. (tr) Alaska Stock. **22** (tcl) PhotoDisc/Getty Images. (tcr) Craig Hosterman/Shutterstock. (tl) Gaertner/Alamy Images. (tr) Potapov Alexander/Shutterstock. **23** Alan D. Carey/PhotoDisc/Getty Images. **24** (br) 8781118005/Shutterstock. (cr) G.K. & Vikki Hart/Photodisc/Getty Images. (t) Creatas/Jupiterimages. **25** DigitalStock/Corbis. **26** (tl) Michael & Patricia Fogden/Minden Pictures/National Geographic Image Collection. (tr) Jill Lang/iStockphoto. **27** Jonathan Blair/National Geographic Image Collection. **28** Olegusk/Shutterstock. **29** Liz Garza Williams/Hampton-Brown/National Geographic School Publishing.

Illustrator Credits
3, **15**, **17**, **29**, **30-31** Aga Kowalski

National Geographic School Publishing
Hampton-Brown
www.NGSP.com

Printed in the USA.
Quad Graphics, Leominster, MA

ISBN: 978-0-7362-8080-8

17 18 19
10 9 8